QUANTUM
HERESIES

To Tracy Smith

In admiration

MARY PEELEN

GLASS LYRE PRESS

Cover Design: JeeneeLeeDesign
Cover Art: Lauren Emmons
Author Photo: Jean-Phillipe Voiron
Design & Layout: Steven Asmussen
Copyediting: Linda E. Kim

Glass Lyre Press, LLC
P.O. Box 2693
Glenview, IL 60025
www.GlassLyrePress.com

QUANTUM HERESIES

MARY PEELEN

Winner of the 2018 Kithara Book Prize

Previous Winners:
2017 – *American Lotus* by Kevin Casey
2016 – *Walking Toward Cranes* by Amy Small-McKinney
2015 – *Ribcage* by Joan Colby
2014 – *Cephalopodic* by J.P. Dancing Bear
2013 – *Idyll for a Vanishing River* by Jeffrey C. Alfier

For Ruby

CONTENTS

I

II

III

QUANTUM HERESIES

I

x

x obeys algebraic laws
but resists particularity.

It's the placeholder
of uncertainty

like the notion of
God.

A variable, a kiss,
a chromosome,

x signs legal documents
in two concise strokes.

It could be me,
you,

or the number of
poppies we planted

out back by the fence
last Sunday.

After so many days of rain,
the afternoon was sunlit,

translucent.
Perfect as an integer.

ZERO

Once
it was nothing—

just a space that ached
like an unmoored ghost,

or antiseptic hours
in a hospital corridor,

aura of *always* and *never*
at the same time.

Then in black and white,
your flesh as a dark bird

aloft in a light box,
forked lines of

an angulated fracture
illuminating the x-rayed sky.

The transformation was
alchemical, your eyes

into plate glass,
black and beady, opiated,

full feathered velocity of
a numeral's first flight.

Supernova

Dying is an art, said Sylvia Plath,
dark energy providing the opposite of gravity.

A future sun will rise up in all its glory
so red and ravenous it devours the daytime sky,

matter ripping itself into sound and light
in one last explosion uncontainable as art itself.

Heaven performs a billion spectacular finales,
it's up to us to conjure the rest.

We'd all start with divinity and work backwards
if we could manage the math

but even Lady Lazarus burned her miraculous hair
in the calculus of resurrection.

Here at the table, event horizon flickering pink,
we begin with the absolute:

the emperor of ice-cream, Mrs. Ramsay's charm,
and light, of course,

the way it always travels at light speed.
Everything else is contingency—

cutlery glinting like a phantom,
peaches in a milk white bowl, figs going bloody blue.

CHAOS THEORY

Entangled in the electromagnetic field
around a human heart,

fate changes its shape recursively.
I learned in childhood

how destiny turns on tiny things,
cracks in the sidewalk, sticks and stones,

apparitions fulfilling the promise
of fundamental symmetry.

It takes an eye for pattern
to see the way the soothsayer sees,

or Mandelbrot, his fractal designs
carving the limits of space.

Galaxies swirl in a teacup,
animals run through pixilated clouds,

new universes like fictions arise
not out of emptiness, but how it's filled

with gravestones and doxologies—
ghost of Grandma P everywhere I look

exhorting me to trust in Jesus,
lorem ipsum of my soul's erratic geometry.

PROGNOSIS

In the long winter of our
histological battle,

blood feuds and the
subsequent insanity,

we call out for the sanctuary
of predictable outcomes

like the parabolic arc
of a free-falling body

like the summer of
rickety wheelbarrows

hauled under the breezeway
that yielded a garden,

wildly fragrant and
resistant to drought.

If cancer strikes you
as random or chaotic,

remember that like
every other algorithm,

it too has a unique function,
the elegance of its own logic.

ONE

Foliage of the Warren pear
is shiny as light.

Red-shifted at dusk,
the sun's last scatter of photons

gathers from each leaf
a thousand shades of green.

Blue jays got the pears
before they were ripe,

pecked them full of holes,
all but one.

Mathematics
can't prove everything.

Gödel proved that some things
are a matter of faith.

When I come to you
offering one small green pear,

I'm asking you to believe in
every green there is,

at every hour.
The whole tree.

FAULT

Bridge to bridge,
the expensive city is

ankle deep in ranunculus
and blue-eyed grass.

Tumbling down Bernal Hill
on a rocky path,

body first,
bewilderment after,

hand in hand, hair aloft,
love laughs in blue jeans

in the afternoon
while the fortunate sun

makes extravagant claims
in the precise hue of oxalis

and California poppies.
On the cliff edge, blackberry

blossoms bruise in the wind,
their fluttery throats

a pink so fragile it
absolves thorns and wickedness.

MIGRAINE

I can't think
about anything else.

Supernova, cataclysm in
the arm of a spiral galaxy,

a great star implodes,
its fiery mass crushed

like a bad draft,
helium into heaviness,

nickel, iron.
Then the explosion—

radioactive,
violently illuminated.

Forging an idea is onerous
as pushing Saturn around

the razored sky
wholly unaided by physics.

Formulae don't apply here,
nor poetry,

no muse has enough gravity.
That's how jealous it is.

THERMODYNAMICS

In the first act of the Anthropocene,
a murder of crows

colors the olive tree
black as widows in a Greek tragedy.

Cursed with that raspy, hideous caw
and a history of intuition,

they lift and scatter as one,
tithing feathers and twigs,

shadow babies left behind writhing
on the flagstone.

Entropy
exacts all manner of atonement,

even the sky recedes in the
shape of an exponential function,

heat longing for something else.
Chaos rises,

the final relic of our creation,
brief and violent as art.

Let it be radiant. Let it be alive.
Give it sharp white teeth.

DRAW

1. ~ lots.

   Given her age and race, the probability was 1 in 70.

2. ~ on her experience.

   In the three weeks leading up to the first surgery, she was
   so anxious she hardly slept or ate. What followed was
   not only worse than she imagined but it lasted forever,
   and so she often thought about those three weeks. She
   could have slept in and eaten ice cream for breakfast. She
   should have taken up fencing and started writing her
   novel.

3. ~ a conclusion.

   The oncologist called her at home on a Sunday evening
   around nine o'clock.

4. ~ a card.

   Years earlier, in India, she'd met a German hippie who
   did a tarot reading for her on the stone floor of a temple
   in Hampi, a holy place known for its caves, scorpions,
   and the local mythology claiming it drives people insane.
   Indeed, she'd seen a crazy woman just that morning—
   wild-haired and half-naked, sari tied around her hips,
   her dark, wrinkled breasts hung nearly to her waist. The
   locals ignored her. She threw cow dung at anyone who
   looked too closely. *You'll be very lucky,* the German hippie
   said, *but first you'll pass through cursed times.*

5. ~ a crowd.

    She received twenty seven flower arrangements and
    nearly a hundred cards and letters.

6. ~ a distinction.

    She noticed the metaphors tended toward the military.
    *The war on. She fought bravely against. After a long battle
    with.* She saw it as more of a surrender. Ativan melting
    on her tongue like a communion wafer, she held out a
    white, sacrificial arm and made her veins permeable to
    their liquid war-lust.

7. ~ fire.

    Inside her bones, caustic as nuclear fuel, something
    secret. Dangerous.

8. ~ the line.

    At the support group, a young woman named Miriam
    said she didn't want a shunt in her head, didn't think it
    would look very good. *Cancer made me a shallower person,*
    she said. They all laughed, Miriam was hilarious; it was
    her timing. Three months later she died.

9. ~ bridge.

Once upon a time, in a castle (of course), under the spell
of a deadly potion (why not?), she slept for a hundred
years. Or a thousand. Nothing could save her. No
Rapunzel's locks—no hair at all, actually—nothing to
span the chasm between our heroine and the real live
world.

10. ~ a blank.

There was something incredibly funny about it,
something she repeated frequently, and when people
were uneasy and didn't know how to console her, she
would say the funny thing, and they would laugh and feel
more comfortable, saying how brave she was, and what a
great attitude she had, but now she can't remember what
it was.

REDSHIFT

I drove west from Michigan
through Illinois, Iowa,

anxious
to reach my Californian destiny

but I paused in Nebraska,
farmland embracing the entire view

the way a magnet
fills space with a force field.

The wind whorled its symmetries
into the Great Plains,

lanky wheat stalks
bending in parallel formation,

vectors gone lithe
in their belonging.

The August sun receded
so charitably over the heartland,

I wonder why it wasn't enough
in wavelength or intensity

to make me someone different.
Lighter.

dx

The scope of the transformation was
infinitesimal. Microscopic, really.

It might have gone undetected
for years except for the way

it altered everything else,
like the way we calculate time.

Instantaneous change isn't derived
by simple addition or subtraction

but a more careful way of
inhabiting the calendar.

Days and hours split apart,
milliseconds subdivide growing

thinner and thinner,
an infinite regression until,

just as the moment collapses
into nothing at all,

it flashes, as brilliant as logic,
a convergence of pinks

overwhelming your forearms—
poppies, penstemon, peonies.

PROPERTIES OF LIGHT

Even in silent observation, she sings,
and ordinary birds

beat their wings in perpetual ceremonies
of freefall and ascension.

Street still dark outside the window,
dimension fills in slowly around

the acacia saplings lined up curbside.
Sparrows leave the earth

in a continuous function,
an oscillation so smooth

it's impossible to analyze
without losing essential data.

Great awakening of a single tree,
black notes lift into blue,

a chaos of semiquavers
struggling to contain divinity.

How eager they are to go on and on,
particles careening in waves,

pressing the fragile air into flight
the way words invent truth in the writing.

APHASIA

It's what you listen for—

the repetition of a word
both noun and verb,

stroke, for example. Or love.
In therapy, my sister

recites her children's names
like a profession of faith.

Afterwards, they disappear
and it's just me again,

benign, vaguely familiar.
I push her chair around

the square glass corridor.
Courtyard snow

melting in the afternoon sun
goes gray around the edges.

Rubber wheels on linoleum
make no sound at all.

PROOF

Despite persistent elements
of planetary suicide

like pesticides and
leaf blowers at seven A.M.,

the cells of the honeycomb
remain perfectly hexagonal.

Jacaranda blooms
festoon the Mission in June

and the ironwoods
branch logarithmically.

A spider web captures prey
in a glory of silken radii.

God is what you believe,
that's the only definition.

It doesn't mean everything
you fear will come to pass.

Amidst daily catastrophe
miracles arise mathematically,

coordinates on a star map
beyond the lure of insanity.

Universal Law

Gravity is the gift of shape,
the downhill way we tend to roll,

so when the bough begins to break,
we know which way to go.

Mass is variable, hard to gauge,
but G is constant,

a glimmering icon
weighty as Grandma P

calling down the Lord at bedtime,
putting us all to shame.

A body at rest
remains at rest,

it's a law of Newtonian motion.
You can trust the math,

so hush now
and let yourself fall.

Lay down your rock-a-bye soul
in the unbounded darkness

where a billion stellar galaxies
unwind their spiraled arms.

II

AWAKE

For Descartes, metaphysics was quick as
a thought, *ergo sum.*

For me, there's Calvinism to consider,
its inbred unworthiness, the voice of my mother,

the moonlight, white and shrill, a migraine aura,
cerebral pomp and ceremony

confounding as transfinite math
or the voice of Rilke's angels in the firmament

luring us toward the end of the number line.
Every infinity is terrifying.

I stammer in the dark, groping for basic Latin,
for Imitrex and acetaminophen,

while outside, over the fence in back,
there's a rake on the roof of the chicken coop.

At dawn, the rooster scuffs the dusty ground
with his flapping red wings.

Neck stretched, combed head tilted back,
he wags his immaculate wattle,

valiantly proclaiming to the dirt yard world
his one, his only truth.

String Theory

From the kitchen window,
the garden hose is a thin green line.

We don't notice the way it curls inside,
hiding more than it shows—

dimension flattens with distance,
like plant matter in the terrible drought.

It's been so hot, Antarctica cracked in two.
I wonder when the panic will set in.

Coiled as secrets inside a marriage,
the earth has interior shape

bound into a space so small
it unites electromagnetism and gravity.

No place for resentment or annoyance,
lies grow white and disappear.

I water the roses and the artichoke,
extravagant, lavender, needier than it looks.

Here at the horizon of theoretical extinction,
we cut flowers for the table.

We sing the way weary mourners do,
praising geometry as if miracles could happen.

Periodic Table of the Elements

OMG we type, and by G
we don't mean what's ineffable.

We mean what's inevitable,
as in gravity or global disaster,

lead in the drinking water,
chromium in the air,

icecaps melting into
floods of Biblical proportion.

We have faith, at least,
that our anxiety is superheavy

as any other element of instability,
copernicium, ununoctium,

large isotopes with nuclei
as weighty as Latin

or the Bishop's golden pyx
carried in full caped procession.

His felted soles on church stone
are crimson, nun-stitched,

subject to the same forces
as all particulate matter.

Birds Of Japan

Binoculars raised, we inspect the sheen of feathers, the curve of a beak, and record the time and date of the backyard sighting on the inside back cover of *Birds of San Francisco* which we keep in the top right-hand drawer in the kitchen.

On NASA's website, a time-lapsed satellite photo of the earth at night. Europe and India are fully illuminated, as is North America, especially New York but most particularly, it's Japan that glows from above—a convergence of neon and incandescent streetlights, headlights, nightlights, flashlights, camera flashes, flashing lights on smoke alarms and teakettles. From outer space Japan radiates, a brilliant star surrounded by seawater.

The BBC reports a major earthquake in Fukushima, damage to the nuclear power plant rumored. Thousands are evacuated, though officials insist there's no public health risk.

Something has to be done. No counter space, no insulation, a broken window, nowhere to put recycling. More than anything in the world, we want a dishwasher. Also one of those spray attachments for the faucet. They look really handy.

Al Jazeera posts early headlines: a tsunami, human toll certain but not quantified, damage from the earthquake undetermined.

We sign with a contractor who uses environmentally-friendly products. The job will be completed in three weeks, and decisions must be made immediately: window cranks, drawer pulls, sink depth, cabinetry, and the shape of ogees. We consider more than forty shades of white paint. It makes us quarrel.

Kitchen walls down to the studs, the house is filthy as a dirt mine. I try to meditate, but I'm afraid, obstructed, air traffic is disrupted. The sky over Japan is emptied of planes, birds, words, paper and that into which it is folded.

Flash of red and an echoless thud—a robin crashes flying into the window. Gray and white feathers quiver on the sill like prayer flags too late. Flapping in the wind, they cover the stoop, the stairs, the sidewalk out front, far more abundance than seems necessary to keep one bird aloft.

Technicians attempting to prevent meltdown are ordered to evacuate the Fukushima power plant.

Outside the kitchen window a chorus of robins erupts in the cherry tree, its blossoms pink and violent as ten thousand hearts breaking open all at once. Online, it's Japan again, spring weather and a plume of toxic wind blowing east by southeast.

The contractor issues another change order. New studs this time. Progress is delayed ten more days, costs exceeding 300% of the original estimate.

Tokyo Electric issues a press release stating they expect a conclusion to the Fukushima nuclear crisis in early October.

We didn't count on the toxicity. A compound used to glue the countertops triggers an intractable migraine. We flee to Paris at the end of our endurance.

There's new construction and from the window of blue room on Passage Sainte-Avoye we no longer witness the swallows' death-defying dives into the cobblestone courtyard, their trust in dusky Parisian air. The way it always lifted them up again.

We lost the bird book, tossed out with all the kitchen rubble, no doubt. We adapt to the new sink depth, but the spray attachment is a disappointment. It never works quite as we imagined.

I fold paper for hours, origami cranes to string along the edge of the radioactive sky.

We can't get over it. We mourn *Birds of San Francisco* like a lost Eden, symbol of something irreparably broken. Something we did wrong.

INFINITE GRAVITY

Bernal Hill is shocking in green.
It rained last night,

violence of a broken truce
after we'd reconciled ourselves to

accelerating drought.
Deep in the core of the galaxy,

there is no doxology, no epiphany,
only a massive black hole,

immeasurable curvature,
a force more powerful than love

spinning in the exquisite blackness
of a suicide.

Dark energy blows the cosmos apart.
The city is in ruins.

Even the birds are mystics—
crows convene on the chimneypiece

predicting unmerciful weather.
Here at the vanguard of apocalypse

the universe is expanding faster than ever.
We're nearly there, water running low.

PROPHECY

O, we'll find someone to blame.
This isn't random.

Chaos is calculable, iterative.
We should have seen it coming.

Afternoon fog obscures Twin Peaks,
verdant fragrance of earth

relinquishing its dominion.
Crows overpopulate San Francisco,

convocations grip the olive tree
in full avian convulsion,

foliage quivering with
the rage of corvid premonition.

Even technology falls away,
nothing but theory remaining.

Mist levitates over the salvia
like a guru demonstrating science.

The second law of thermodynamics
promises entropy for every creature

no matter how darkly feathered.
No matter how guilty.

VOCATION

Ah, to iron wholly
for the sanctity of creases

or to weep purely,
as if for the love of a hankie.

But there's always
something at stake—

time, money,
a metaphor.

Here, for example,
this daily admonishment:

three cereal boxes
on the kitchen countertop,

all of them open
and nearly empty.

Putting them away
would

signify
my discipline.

Leaving them there
means I have none.

ONTOLOGY

The window frame goes pop
shirking the cold of the night,

a brand new crack
in the fundamental code.

Emptiness is highly unstable.
An earthquake, an aftershock,

a startle response—
random flux is all it takes.

Hair-triggered, neuralgia
sends a metal zip down my spine,

chronic, seismic.
California forks at the fault-line

while in the lacy dendrites
of my sympathetic nerve,

impulses fire as faithfully
as any branch of mathematics.

Tined, ionized, they breach
the ethereal frequencies,

proof of a small god
with a high tolerance for tedium.

Aurora Borealis

Far north,
a reckoning in the neon sky

blinding as an ocular migraine,
its taste of iron on the tongue.

In the nearly breathable
realms of the atmosphere,

solar winds animate
the earth's polar flowlines,

magnetic pole gone glinty
with the static of old ghosts.

Oxygen and nitrogen collide,
charged particles ignite,

green and violet night-flares
reach toward heaven

like arms of the reclaimed
at the rapture.

Neurological sequelae
caustic as Arctic weather

call for lurid belief
as the means of salvation.

BIOPSY

The pathology report is
a column of pure mathematics

paradoxical
as the double-slit experiment.

Surgeon's knife sliced
the x of a cicatrix

dividing flesh
from its miscalculation,

nerves and vanity
split apart like

photons
into wave and particle.

The procedure was painless,
monstrous. Fully ritualized.

Now it's thin, a page of numbers
and a smile of white skin

numb as Novocain,
ghastly row of sutured teeth

biting through
the anesthetized plane.

THE BIG BANG

Psalm of a million tiny moments,
the fundamental theorem of calculus

unites every x from zero to infinity.
Oncology requires the same kind of faith.

We stretch out our arms and run blindly,
summing at full tilt as we go,

measuring cells, even as they subdivide
to isolate an element of truth

so small as to be perfectly inconsequential.
After the great catastrophe

angels sang in the pitch of faraway heavens,
dust spun into moons and meteorites,

trace elements forged into artifacts—
two ticket stubs, a house-key,

a scarlet dress with a train,
olive trees pruned in the moonlight.

The surgeon cites statistics like a rosary
while we take meticulous notes,

our universe expanding
with dazzling new pathologies.

STAGECRAFT

Dramatis Personæ: Humor the ghost that haunts you. Let's say her name is Jane. Close your eyes for a moment, entertain the idea. You can play the other character. You're a white woman, age thirty to forty-five, fatigued lately, perfect for the role.

Stage Directions: Wait expectantly in the dark, and when the curtain rises, permit the full contraction of your throat. Thus honed, your attention will animate the actors in the exact same way a planchette glides across the Ouija board when poised between reverent fingertips. C - A - N - C - E - R it spells out slowly, though far too early in the play.

Synopsis: The drama will unfold exactly as you might expect, three acts, a rise and fall in the action, heroine, villain, curtain call. Right on cue at age thirty-five, Jane is diagnosed. Your fate will remain unknown until the very last scene, but don't be afraid to go onstage. You must go on. Who else is there to speak for the dead? All they ask is that you perform your lowly pageant, drink the poison, wear all their pink crap. Don a wig.

Set: A lightbulb hangs from an infinitely long wire over a black stage. When you look closely, you see Jane curled up around the filament like a tiny fetus. *I have an idea,* she whispers.

Prologue: Platitudes delivered by the Jester, the Gravedigger, or the Voice of God, as technology allows.

Act One: Imagine you're a woman who always knows what to say. (Don't worry, everyone pretends. It's acting.) At the hospital, follow the narrow, concrete stairway down to the place beneath logic, to the platform of your empty heart. Ignore the weepy Hallmark indignities and go ahead. Emote. On that spot-lit expanse, you'll become a strange kind of star, hairless and humiliated.

Act Two: Dialog is careful, hushed, deadly serious. Or else it's overly cheerful. Pay attention to the subtext. With the aid of morphine, you'll hear them from the wings—voices prompting you with lines you'll need later, like *Stage 2* and *probability of metastasis*.

Act Three: No magic words can make the dark smudge on Jane's CT scan disappear. She's trapped in Stage 4, while you walk free, no less guilty, just luckier. Promise you'll see her again. Swear you'll bring flowers, Chapstick, magazines, Xanax, anything it takes. Then before it's too late, turn and run. *Run.* Do it now. Find a disguise, become someone else, change your wig and phone number. Do not allow yourself to be typecast.

Epilogue: Jane exits more suddenly than expected, drives herself to the emergency room and expires right there on the floor. Clap politely before you stand up and collect your things. Out in the lobby, tighten your raincoat before you step back into the street.

PRIME

Forty one apples in the tree,
red and round,

praise awaiting gravity,
wholly free of abstraction.

When it comes to the primes
and matters of religion,

I defer to Pythagoras,
his ancient cult and authority.

Deep in the rites of spring
he reveled in geometry,

the shape of the soul,
the promise of reincarnation,

form and emptiness at play
in the purest recreation.

Sun-ripened, fragrant,
apples offer up a real number,

two score and one, twin prime
fallen in a curious distribution

beautiful as conjecture
on this fault-riven ground.

PLANE GEOMETRY

Perfectly round and chemically green,
corn crops inscribe the plains.

In 14B, a woman is reading a mystery,
a genre popular on airplanes—

death enlarges the scope things,
including one's sense of legroom.

Once, from a rocky lunar overlook,
astronauts saw the first earthrise,

new blue world making its elliptical pass
through a sky unbounded as fiction.

Jane Austen saw it coming all along.
Like every point in the universe,

her parlor was center of the star chart.
Even here, Miss Bennett and her sisters

define the arc of a narrative structure
in the precise shape of my flight home.

Far below, sunlit
lines of concrete bisect the desert

tracing a straight-edge all the way
to the origin.

INTERIM

If beauty can be salvaged,
it must.

Headache coming on early,
I stand in the dark

and trim the weary tulips,
plunging stems

like knives into the cut
glass vase by the sink.

The countertop is marble,
exquisitely geologic—

perfection was attainable
in the Paleozoic age.

I bend at the knee,
turn my head to the side,

and slowly apply
my pulsing temporal vein

to the mausoleum stone,
smooth and cool as logic.

It's time that strands us here.
We wait for it. It takes so long.

CONFESSIONS

—in memory of Tom Andrews (1961 – 2001)

Once I knew a smart boy who thought I was stupid.
He wrote poetry about Augustine, and then he died,

a hemophiliac, his bloody joints steeped in codeine,
liver cells swollen as semicolons.

Motocross was his roaring act of self-defiance.
He popped wheelchair wheelies,

shredded the dirt-bike earth into a fine body of light,
diaries rendered in typeset glory

while his mother begged forgiveness
for the sin of her blue blood womb.

Death in his back pocket,
he traded fate like baseball cards

in the wormy backyard of a Michigan summer.
Fraternal blood bond, his brother went first,

same year I met him.
I'm still here, readjusting the clench of my jaw,

reading St. Augustine on the futility of prayer,
on eternity, how it never gives in,

guilty of finding
stupidity where a smart boy saw only God.

FORTUNE

Here in the palm of my hand,
a lifeline, sign of what's promised:

a feel for logarithmic logic
and the erosion of Ocean Beach.

Granular, geologic, California
cracks at the coastline

etching its fractal designs
at every scale of magnification.

Sand blows like snow
across Great Highway.

Gripped in my fist, it falls
as waterfalls.

Counting on my fingers, I
ritualize the power of ten.

The great catastrophe is underway,
dissolution coming in waves.

Here at the left-hand limit of America
the seawater rises to meet us.

Fissures in the ice-lip of Antarctica
keen, their tone deepening every day.

III

Genesis

We met in a concrete cinema.
I'd been waiting there forever.

In the beginning
was a burst of cosmic inflation,

creation of a universe
at the speed of light squared—

emptiness was made into
time and space at every location.

Quantum gravity pressed the map
with celestial curves

smooth as seduction
to draw the falling planets in.

After nine billion years
the Earth began to spin.

Velocity was instantaneous.
She arrived late, of course,

bearing armloads of snapdragons
wrapped in newspaper,

golden blossoms the color of
light becoming new.

Sunday Morning

In the last shower of summer days,
I stand at the window

fixing distances in the air,
claiming the limits of my knowledge.

Scrub jays tryst in the fig tree,
hummingbirds spar in flashes of neon armor.

The Fuji apple tree espaliered to the fence
at the back of the garden

fruits miraculously in the city fog.
Long exhausted of flowery white,

leafed branches curve into
ten dimensions so discrete

we'd miss them entirely
if not for the math.

I put my faith in algebra.
And Wallace Stevens, of course,

his quantum heresies, his dominion,
coffee and oranges,

birds defying gravity,
theory contained in a curved glass jar.

Negative One

Hideous shriek of a windstorm
sends the jacaranda

scraping against
the fence out back.

With every gust
the flesh of the trunk is gouged,

sliced in the shape of
an axillary scar.

We wait until dusk
and then, cruel as heroics,

we fetch the lopper
from the shed,

extend its arm to grip
the offending branch,

metal jaw biting through
bark and pith.

The limb drops,
a negative progression,

the way we counted surgeries
in a year of bad weather.

Probability

Graduation night was overwrought
as heat lightning

in a sky so charged with electrons
we nearly burst into flame.

Optimistic as Midwestern girls,
we dreamt of quantum entanglement,

our cliquish leap into brilliance
about as likely as photon emission.

Dust drew into storm clouds,
trace minerals mingled with possibility,

elementary particles dashed in and out
making their statistical appearances.

1 over 137. The odds were against us.
Two suicides that year. A car wreck.

A few girls got pregnant. Some got away.
All the usual forces applied:

money, guilt, electromagnetic charm.
Only the numbers were predictable,

and the weather, a sky rolling in
raindrops that were perfectly round.

QUANTUM BEHAVIOR

Electricity skittered over the lake
of asphalt behind the high school,

heat lightning flashed from
cloud to cloud, virtual particles

tracing Feynman diagrams
across the ciphered sky.

The air was ionized, charged
as an August night in Michigan,

ninety, humid,
cicadas screaming bloody murder.

We all had premonitions then—
all our energy was potential,

uncertainty was our own invention,
brand new as sex or sin.

In our kinetic futures
we'd smooth our staticky hair,

damning ourselves to
predictability.

HEMICRANIA

Highly sensitive to initial conditions,
her narrow hips went frigid, iron-rigid

on the steps behind the swimming pool,
icicles sharpening the tips of her hair

while other girls dispersed into
carpools out across the icy parking lot.

The cement was cold and municipal,
pedestal of the great divide.

The headache would come later,
one-sided, hallucinatory.

Peripheral darkness pressed in at first,
crushing the cold into crystals of air.

Tinnitus rang
concentric haloes of silver and white,

herald of the full ocular eclipse,
bright points of blue stabbing through.

The ceremony was electrical, hormonal.
Fully definitional.

Cerebral fissure: the abyss between
two halves of the brain.

BAROMETER

I skied downhill in the dark
white Michigan woods

frictionless as a vector,
exhilarated

with velocity,
magnitude, and direction,

my hair aloft in the frigid air,
long tail of the arrow.

As in all creation myths,
the details were biological:

a cranium, a sassafras tree.
The moon was astrological.

The collision was random
as any subatomic event.

Its effect was small at first,
evolving in complexity and

technical precision.
Migraine as meteorology.

Symptoms are quantifiable
when a storm is on the way.

ORIGIN

When first introduced
to the Cartesian plane

we fell in love
with the concept of ordered pairs.

Math makes the world predictable
but weather is more adverbial.

It was insanely stormy that night,
howling wind

and terribly late,
a ridiculous hour

to drive across the Bay Bridge
to see a grainy old movie about

animals running in the wild
and yet within

the fixed parameters
of grammar and cinematography

it was our only axis of intersection.
I knew right away—

we'd arrived at a unique solution.
Time reset to zero.

UNIFIED THEORY

Here in the dark, we await the alignment
of Mars and a blood red moon

while an iris blooms in a cut glass vase
in perfect three-sided symmetry.

We argued tonight, our rhetoric elliptical,
careful distance a constant.

Oh, how I long for an elegant solution,
a truce with margin for error.

An olive branch scratches
the window screen in the wind,

a sign of the forces that bind us:
the strong, the weak, electromagnetic,

gravity still out there in
the zodiacal blue, beguiling as

a muezzin's call from a far minaret
harkening to collapsing bodies,

to planets, to distant suns and satellites,
to you and me, love,

our wobbling orbit longing for shape
in the quiver of morning.

URSA MAJOR

—in memory of Margaret Miller (1963 — 2017)

The building is shrouded in scaffolding.
Dirge of the jackhammer begins at nine.

Faith is squandered on religion—
it's harder to believe in teeth and bones,

the soul's earthly heft
so blithely fractured.

Margaret had a light about her
alluring as a beacon. Or a drug.

Once, feigning hypothermia
for a search-and-rescue class,

she nearly died out in the wild.
Half covered in twigs and leaves,

as if in hibernation, she lay so still
the students failed to find her.

I shiver on my city balcony
below the sharp rime star,

pockmarked cement gone lunar gray.
I can't pray anymore.

I can't bear the blaze of this asterism
spread out across the ruthless sky.

LOGICAL POSITIVISM

Perpetually under surveillance,
New York shimmers in halogen,

gaudy windows lined up
in the high-rise across the street.

My cabdriver said traffic moves
sadly since the election.

When the rogue rain stops,
garbage trucks yawn and roar.

Down in the subway, train tracks
shriek in parallel vibrato,

American anxiety accelerating
in both directions at once.

Upstairs at Bleecker Street station,
the usual infinities:

concrete and construction bins,
begging bowls alongside

all the gilded excess of Broadway.
When the lights go out

only philosophers will dance
on these highly examined rooftops.

Heaven & Hell: The Visible Spectrum

Red

We place sugary trumpets between our lips, salvia blossoms plucked from our San Francisco garden. Wildly territorial, a hummingbird descends, hovering. We stand motionless while it brazenly kisses our mouths—hers then mine—its jeweled gorget flashing, invisible wings slicing the air into light.

On Andros in Greece, mosquitoes swarm in the night. We can't sleep—slapping, scratching, cursing, weeping, so exhausted we're crazy with it, ears buzzing, the white-washed walls of our room splattered with mayhem in the morning.

Orange

My first infinity was a stretch of summer in Grand Haven when I wasn't obliged to account for my time nor the dunes of sand in my hair. Every evening Lake Michigan reflected the penitent sky, its glorious banner proclaiming the end of things.

I stop for gas in Muskegon where a man is helping himself to beef jerky from a jar on the counter. A billion photons ricochet off his hunting jacket, neon assault as brutal and persistent as mythology, an ancient story of headaches and unavenged crime.

Yellow

We're nearly to Andros when a hole the size of a coin opens in the low and endless sky, and a perfect fortune glances off the Aegean in both wave and particle.

From goat-crossed Kalivari we view the daily procession of oil tankers from Izmir—silent, flagged, stately. Froth laps the shore in their wake depositing a filmy tar that stains the sun-bleached marble.

Green

Secretly, Ruby was obsessed with Catholicism and martyrs. Jewish schoolgirl reciting her Greek and Latin, she pressed pleats of black watch plaid between her fingers luxuriating in a feel for the occult.

Ruby rolls over, looks outside at the olive tree. *I used to be jealous,* she says. *What?* I sit up. *When?* I prod, I insist, but she won't tell me what she means. Just some nonsense about Sappho. How she was always fragmentary.

Blue

The sea glimmers from every direction. The breeze in Andros is scented with wild thyme, goatherds call in their flocks at dusk, and Ruby forgets to regret she's turning fifty.

Ruby's cranky, says, *you write about migraines too much.* Bruised, guilty, headache tangled in my hair, I swear I'll never write another word as long as I live.

Indigo

The wine-dark sea is velvety and complex with pinks and azure.
I can swim forever, fantastically buoyant, utterly confident of my
breaststroke.

The car ferry back to Rafina is rusty, ancient with smells of oil
and frightened people. Everyone's sent down below in the storm,
Captain's orders.

Violet

Twin Peaks is antennaed, touching a sky precisely the color of
home on a jetlagged evening. We were in the air forever.

Outside in the hot sun all day long, we were night-gowned, thirsty,
barefoot as Greek statues. We'd stepped outside to see the very last
rosy-fingered dawn, and the door locked shut behind us.

First Person

Contrivance of
scribes and bridge builders

i is impeccable
when it comes to the math

but it's more dodgy
metaphysically speaking,

not even real,
a magician's apparition

soaring unhindered
in the conceptual remove.

Square root of negative one,
i defines the complex plane.

Pythagoras made it mystical
to keep it inaccessible—

he feared its exposure
would unmake the world.

Curse of the memoir,
start of a lie, fiction's darling,

extra-geometric, *i*
with the power of mutability.

ALGEBRA

Trying to outrun the problem,
I'm open to suggestion,

to opiates, my skin to scalpel edges.
I alter my velocity,

my location from *a* to *b*,
from Paris to Grand Rapids, say,

where, caffeinated and vaguely dizzy,
I watch luggage circling on a belt.

Jetlag comes and goes, wavelike
as chronic illness

distorting the shape of the room.
The airport

is the same as O'Hare, same shops,
same worries: time and money.

I like to think I'm gaining ground,
correcting miscalculations,

until I see my new path
conforms to the same old equation,

slope—rise over run—identical
to the original at every single point.

HYPOTENUSE

We stood at her window
and watched it fall,

slow
as a protracted illness.

Call of the white wood
was long and shrill,

sinews of
cambium stretching.

Reverence is instinctual for
that which is cyclical—

tides, the souls of wildfowl,
Saturn's howling return.

Her skull receded in phases,
powdery, lunar.

We saw it coming.
Time had been a smooth curve

until the ash tree fell,
square root, sum of the squares,

brave new measure
spanning the backyard stream.

REMAINDER

They each say it unprompted:
Toni at school who never says such things,

Juan from Taco Loco,
the guy loitering in front of McDonald's,

even the mailman on Mission Street,
deep in his afternoon alcoholism—

Hey! That coat is nice! as if
it's the only thing in the world to say.

Nothing special about it though,
cut of an ordinary garment.

It's her.
Needle thin, she threaded herself

through a blanket of morphine and
bequeathed to me her final word,

at peace with the fragrance of
Salem Lights, cool and minty forever.

Now she rides the weave of black wool.
How she shimmers,

hangs onto shiny things, buttons and fire.
Looks good on me.

REMEMBRANCE

Since the construction out back,
the birds are gone from the Marais courtyard

and I can't read this long book anymore.
Proust imperils time.

Here, in the blue room on rue Rambuteau,
I work methodically,

plotting points to reconstruct the past:
a madeleine, a cork-lined room,

rooftop view from the skylight
upstairs in the chambre de bonne,

swallows swooping like bell curves at dusk,
their perpetual submission to gravity

conferring transcendence.
The weary bells of St. Eustache peal on and on

while I write down all the gods I can remember
and which tea cakes they like to eat.

For a long time, then, and really quite early,
light plays on the pigmented wall, a nightfall

as capacious and smooth as upholstery
drawing my fragile body into itself.

Mandelbrot Set

From outer space, the earth is
a discrete blue globe,

the sun, a single pixel in the
widescreen version of heaven.

It's only up close
that the world goes on forever.

Euclid loved a perfect sphere
but geometry grows old, now,

and the orb isn't round anymore.
Here at Ocean Beach, the length

of our stroll increases without limit
the more persistently we measure it.

Stones crack recursively
from stars into fragments

hewn to an edge, infinitely long,
aggressively unsanded.

The wide, white Pacific tide erodes
a sea cliff at the edge of the city—

echo eternal as a god
returning the same beautiful equation.

VARIABLE

The *x* could have been
anything at all,

the sound of wind chimes,
a gong, a choir, a cantor,

a mermaid, a schoolmarm,
cathedral bells.

Instead — what a lark —
it's laughter.

The man who sits
in the park across the street

has habits of hilarity
disciplined as a cleric,

ha exhaled in eight pulses,
stress on the third and fifth,

never the slightest flux
in rhythm, volume, or pitch.

His breath orders the world
into countable sets,

number expressed as a verb.
It calls me back.

ACKNOWLEDGMENTS

My gratitude to the editors of the journals in which these poems first appeared:

Alaska Quarterly Review ("Universal Law," "dx," "x")

Antioch Review ("Periodic Table of the Elements")

Baltimore Review ("Interim")

Barrow Street Journal ("Properties of Light," "Prophecy")

Beloit Poetry Journal ("Aphasia")

Bennington Review ("Draw")

Deaf Poets Society ("Aurora Borealis," "Barometer")

Dunes Review ("Quantum Behavior")

Guesthouse ("Negative One")

Harvard Divinity Bulletin ("One," "Prognosis")

Journal of Humanistic Mathematics ("First Person," "Algebra," "Prime," "Plane Geometry")

The Massachusetts Review ("Variable")

Michigan Quarterly Review ("Migraine," "Zero")

the minnesota review ("Confessions")

New American Writing ("Fault," "Remembrance")

Pleiades ("Ontology")

Poetry Review (UK) ("String Theory," "Awake")

Psaltery & Lyre ("Proof," "Sunday Morning")

Radar Poetry ("Thermodynamics," "Chaos Theory," "Mandelbrot Set," "Infinite Gravity," "Probability," "Supernova")

Tinderbox Poetry Journal ("Birds of Japan")

Valparaiso Poetry Review ("Hemicrania")

"Stagecraft" appeared in *The Shell Game: Writers Play with Borrowed Forms.* Kim Adrian, ed. University of Nebraska Press, 2018.

"Aphasia" was featured by *Poetry Daily*.

My deep thanks to the poets and artists who supported the creation of this book:

Monica Regan, Toni Mirosevich, Jennifer Sweeney, Susan Rich, Leila Chatti, Elizabeth Bradfield, Amanda Davidson, Brian Thorstenson, Frances Phillips, Onnesha Roychoudhuri, Marco Lean, Shruti Swamy, Mandy Dowd, Leslie Adrienne Miller, Laura Horn, Maxine Chernoff, Lynn Hershman-Leeson, Catherine Wagner, Loretta Gargan, Charlotta Westergren, Anisse Gross, Tony Safford, Anna Hawkins, and Catherine Zimmer.

Special thanks to Laura Robinson and Imee Millado of the BLC.

These poems were scientifically informed and creatively inspired by the books and articles of these geniuses: Alan Lightman, Rebecca Goldstein, Janna Levin, Brian Greene, James Gleick, Michio Kaku, Leonard Susskind, Natalie Wolchover, John Barrow, Carlo Rovelli, and Lisa Randall. Thank you.

I'm grateful to my parents, Allyn Peelen, Esther Ross and Richard B. Ross.

Many thanks to Ami Kaye, Kelly Cressio-Moeller, and Steven Asmussen at Glass Lyre Press for choosing this book and ushering it into the world. Thank you to Jeenee Lee for the cover design.

Most especially, with all my heart, thank you B. Ruby Rich. For everything.

ABOUT THE AUTHOR

Mary Peelen was born and raised in Michigan. She studied mathematics as an undergraduate then traveled widely before completing an M.Div. at the Graduate Theological Union and an M.F.A. in creative writing at San Francisco State University. She lives in San Francisco and Paris.

Her poetry, fiction, and nonfiction have appeared in *Interim, Gulf Coast, Redivider, Alaska Quarterly Review, Antioch Review, Bennington Review, Michigan Quarterly Review, Harvard Divinity Bulletin, Crab Creek Review, Beloit Poetry Journal, Poetry Review (UK),* and other journals.

Glass Lyre Press

exceptional works to replenish the spirit

Glass Lyre Press is an independent literary publisher interested in technically accomplished, stylistically distinct, and original work. Glass Lyre seeks diverse writers that possess a dynamic aesthetic and an ability to emotionally and intellectually engage a wide audience of readers.

Glass Lyre's vision is to connect the world through language and art. We hope to expand the scope of poetry and short fiction for the general reader through exceptionally well-written books, which evoke emotion, provide insight, and resonate with the human spirit.

Poetry Collections
Poetry Chapbooks
Select Short & Flash Fiction
Anthologies

www.GlassLyrePress.com

9 781941 783559